A Beginning-to-Read Book

Let's Play Basketball

by Mary Lindeen

NORWOOD HOUSE PRESS

DEAR CAREGIVER, The *Beginning to Read—Read and Discover* books provide emergent readers the opportunity to explore the world through nonfiction while building early reading skills. The text integrates both common sight words and content vocabulary. These key words are featured on lists provided at the back of the book to help your child expand his or her sight word recognition, which helps build reading fluency. The content words expand vocabulary and support comprehension.

Nonfiction text is any text that is factual. The Common Core State Standards call for an increase in the amount of informational text reading among students. The Standards aim to promote college and career readiness among students. Preparation for college and career endeavors requires proficiency in reading complex informational texts in a variety of content areas. You can help your child build a foundation by introducing nonfiction early. To further support the CCSS, you will find Reading Reinforcement activities at the back of the book that are aligned to these Standards.

Above all, the most important part of the reading experience is to have fun and enjoy it!

Sincerely,

Shannon Cannon

Shannon Cannon, Ph.D.
Literacy Consultant

Norwood House Press • P.O. Box 316598 • Chicago, Illinois 60631
For more information about Norwood House Press please visit our website at www.norwoodhousepress.com or call 866-565-2900.
© 2016 Norwood House Press. Beginning-to-Read™ is a trademark of Norwood House Press. All rights reserved. No part of this book may be reproduced or utilized in any form or by any means without written permission from the publisher.

Editor: Judy Kentor Schmauss
Designer: Lindaanne Donohoe

Photo Credits:

Shutterstock, cover, 3 (NaturSport), 6-7 (Matthew Jacques), 8-9 (Domenic Gareri), 12-13 (Aspen Photo), 14 (photofriday), 14 inset (Pukhoc Konstantin), 15 (Rob van Esch), 16-17 (Richard Paul Kane), 18-19 (Aspen Photo),20 (Chris Minor), 21 (Christopher Halloran), 22-23 (efecreata media group), 26-27, 28-29; Dreamstime, 1 (©Stephanie Swartz), 4-5 (©monkeybusinessimages), 24-25 (©Larisap)

Library of Congress Cataloging-in-Publication Data
Lindeen, Mary.
Lets play basketball / by Mary Lindeen.
  pages cm. – (A Beginning to Read Book)
  Summary: "Basketball is a team sport that is played on a court. The players wear uniforms and try to get the ball through the hoop at the end of the court. Find out about the coach, making points, and how to win a game. This title includes reading activities and a word list"– Provided by publisher.
  Audience: K to Grade 3.
  ISBN 978-1-59953-685-9 (Library Edition : alk. paper)
  ISBN 978-1-60357-770-0 (eBook)
  1. Basketball–Juvenile literature. I. Title. II. Title: Let us play basketball!
  GV885.1.L4946 2015
  796.323–dc23
                        2014047620

Manufactured in the United States of America in Stevens Point, Wisconsin. 275N–062015

Each team has its
own uniform.

Each player has
a number.

These people are playing basketball.
It is a team sport.

Each team also has
a coach.

The coach helps the
team play together
better.

You play basketball on a court.

The court has a hoop at each end.

It is up high.

Each team tries to
get the ball through
their hoop.

The other team tries
to stop them.

Players run up and
down the court.

They go from one
end to the other.

They jump with the ball.
They bounce the ball.

They throw the ball.

Referees make sure
the players follow
the rules.

This player makes
a basket!

He gets the ball
through the hoop!

His team will get
points.

NATIONAL INVITATION
TOURNAMENT

CLEMSON

00.0   PERIOD 2

BELMONT

73

7   TM FOULS   8

68

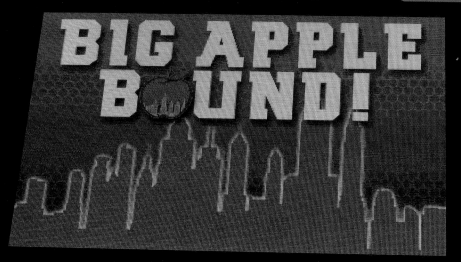

The scoreboard shows
the points for each team.

The team with the
most points wins.

You can play basketball inside.

It can be a big game.

You can play
outside.

It can be a small
game.

All you need is a
basketball and
a hoop . . .

And some friends!

Have fun!

·· Reading Reinforcement ··

CRAFT AND STRUCTURE

To check your child's understanding of this book, recreate the following diagram on a sheet of paper. Read the book with your child, then help him or her fill in the diagram using what they learned. Work together to complete the diagram by stating what he or she already knows about basketball, what he or she wants to know, and what he or she learned from reading this book:

What I Know

What I Want to Know

What I Learned

VOCABULARY: Learning Content Words

Content words are words that are specific to a particular topic. All of the content words for this book can be found on page 32. Use some or all of these content words to complete one or more of the following activities:

- As you write a content word, scramble the order of the letters. Give your child a definition of the word. Have him or her use the definition and the letters to guess the word. Ask him or her to unscramble the letters to spell the word correctly.

- Help your child make up sentences that use two or more content words.

- Make up a story together using as many of the content words as you can.

- Say a content word. Have your child say the first word that comes to his or her mind. Discuss connections between the two words.

- Help your child make up riddles for which content words are the answers.

FOUNDATIONAL SKILLS: *r*-Controlled vowels

When a vowel (*a, e, i, o, u*) comes before the letter *r*, the sound of the vowel changes. This is called an *r*-controlled vowel. Have your child identify the *r*-controlled vowels in the list below. Then ask your child to find words with *r*-controlled vowels in this book.

bounce	friends	sure
better	players	rules
court	scoreboard	sport

CLOSE READING OF INFORMATIONAL TEXT

Close reading helps children comprehend text. It includes reading a text, discussing it with others, and answering questions about it. Use these questions to discuss this book with your child:

- What is a coach's job?
- What does a basketball look like?
- How does a player score points in basketball?
- How is basketball similar to another game you like to play?
- What would happen if a hoop didn't have a net on it?
- Would it be better if basketball hoops were lower to the ground? Why or why not?

FLUENCY

- Reread this book to your child at least two times while he or she uses a finger to track each word as you read it.
- Read the first sentence aloud. Then have your child reread the sentence with you. Continue until you have finished this book.
- Ask your child to read aloud the words they know on each page of this book. (Your child will learn additional words with subsequent readings.)
- Have your child practice reading this book several times to improve accuracy, rate, and expression.

••• Word List •••

Let's Play Basketball uses the 79 words listed below. *High-frequency* words are those words that are used most often in the English language. They are sometimes referred to as sight words because children need to learn to recognize them automatically when they read. *Content words* are any words specific to a particular topic. Regular practice reading these words will enhance your child's ability to read with greater fluency and comprehension.

High-Frequency Words

a	each	high	other	they
all	end	his	own	this
also	for	is	people	through
and	from	it	show(s)	to
are	get(s)	its	small	together
at	go	make(s)	some	up
be	has	most	the	will
big	have	number	their	, with
can	he	on	them	you
down	help(s)	one	these	

Content Words

ball	court	inside	referees	sure
basket	follow	jump	rules	team
basketball	friends	need	run	throw
better	fun	outside	scoreboard	tries
bounce	game	play(er, ers, ing)	sport	uniform
coach	hoop	points	stop	wins

••• About the Author

Mary Lindeen is a writer, editor, parent, and former elementary school teacher. She has written more than 100 books for children and edited many more. She specializes in early literacy instruction and books for young readers, especially nonfiction.

••• About the Advisor

Dr. Shannon Cannon is a teacher educator in the School of Education at UC Davis, where she also earned her Ph.D. in Language, Literacy, and Culture. She serves on the clinical faculty, supervising pre-service teachers and teaching elementary methods courses in reading, effective teaching, and teacher action research.